WENDY PIRK

iThink Books

The Cat Family

All cat species, domestic and wild, are part of the Feline family (Felidae). They all have a common ancestor.

Cats are native to every continent except Australia and Antarctica.

Domestication

Q. Where do cats like to go on field trips?

A. To the meow-seum.

Cats first became pets in Ancient Egypt. Wild cats hunted the mice, rats and snakes that damaged the Egyptian's crops. This helped the people, so they fed the cats special treats, like fish, and gave them shelter so they would stay around. Over time, the cats became pets.

Cats were so special in ancient Egypt that they were thought to be the property of the pharaoh.

It was against the law to hurt or kill a cat, even by accident. The punishment for harming a cat was death.

The oldest breed of domestic cat could be the Egyptian mau. It looks like the cats you see in ancient Egyptian art.

Lions

Lions are the only cats that live in groups. Most cats live alone once they are adults.

The male lion is the only cat that has a mane.

Famous Wild Cousins

Tiger

The tiger is the largest member of the cat family. It lives in Asia.

The Canadian lynx has huge feet that act like snowshoes to help it move around in deep snow.

Lynx

Q. What does the lioness say to the rest of the pride before they go out to hunt?

A. Let us prey.

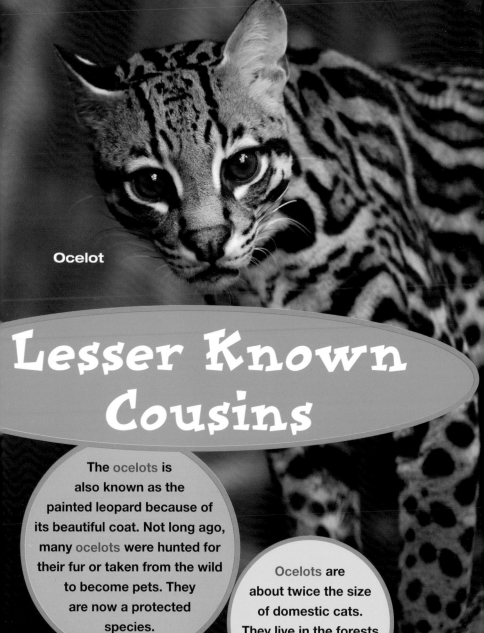

Ocelot

Lesser Known Cousins

The ocelots is also known as the painted leopard because of its beautiful coat. Not long ago, many ocelots were hunted for their fur or taken from the wild to become pets. They are now a protected species.

Ocelots are about twice the size of domestic cats. They live in the forests of central and South America.

The sand cat lives in the deserts of northern Africa and Asia.

It has fur on the bottom of its feet to protect its paws from the hot sand.

Sand Cat

The serval lives on the African savannah. It is sometimes called the giraffe cat because of its super long legs. It also has the biggest ears for its body size of any cat.

Serval

The serval can stand on its hind legs and jump straight up in the air to grab birds flying by.

Q. How do you make a serval disappear?

A. With spot remover!

Most common breeds

There are more than 40 purebred breeds of domestic cat. To be a purebred, a cat's parents must both be the same breed.

Cats that are not purebred are put into one of three groups: domestic shorthair, domestic longhair or domestic medium hairs.

Domestic Longhair

Only 1 in 10 cats is a longhair.

Domestic Shorthair

The **domestic shorthair** is one of the most common breeds in the world.

Q. Why was the cat sent to the principal's office?

A. She was a cheetah!

Calico **cats have blocks of white, orange and black fur.**

Tabbies **are the most common cats. They have striped coats.**

Colour patterns

Tortoiseshells also have a mix of red and black, and sometimes white, but the colours are swirled together instead of in blocks.

Solid **coats** are all one colour.

Q. What is a cat's favourite colour?

A. Purr-ple!

Biggest breeds

Maine
Coon

A male Maine coon can weigh as much as 25 pounds (11.3 kg). Females are a bit smaller, up to 20 pounds (9 kg).

The "coon" part of their name comes from the bushy tail, which often has rings, like a racoon's.

Q. What do you call a pile of cats?

A. A meow-tain!

Ragdoll

The ragdoll is another big cat, only slightly smaller than the Maine coon.

It is called the ragdoll because it lets its body go limp when it is picked up. It goes all droopy just like a rag doll.

Although it has a thick coat, the ragdoll does not shed much.

Smallest breeds

Singapura

The singapura is the smallest breed of cat. It weighs about 6 pounds (2.7 kg.), the same as 3 guinea pigs.

Some people think the smallest breed is the Russian toybob. When it is full grown, this tiny cat is the size of a regular 4-month-old kitten. Not everyone believes this cat is a true breed.

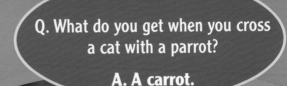

Q. What do you get when you cross a cat with a parrot?

A. A carrot.

Corish Rex

The Cornish Rex is another small breed, weighing about as much as 4 guinea pigs.

Most types of cat have 3 layers of fur in their coat, but the Cornish Rex has only the bottom layer. Its fur is short, wavy and super soft.

Bengal

Some domestic cat breeds are a mix of domestic and wild cat.

The bengal is a cross between an Asian leopard cat and domestic cat.

Its coat can have "rosettes" (spots with a dark outline) like a jaguar, or spots, like a leopard.

Wildest breeds

Peterbald cats can have different levels of hairlessness. Some are completely bald with skin that feels like leather; some are fuzzy like the sphynx; and others may have tufts of fur on their feet, face or tail.

If hairless cats go outside, they need sunscreen to protect them from getting a sunburn.

Peterbald Cats

Hairless cats

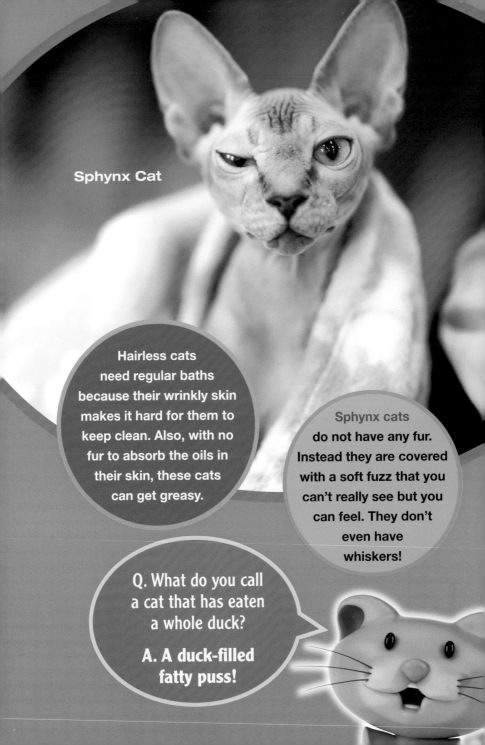

Sphynx Cat

Hairless cats need regular baths because their wrinkly skin makes it hard for them to keep clean. Also, with no fur to absorb the oils in their skin, these cats can get greasy.

Sphynx cats do not have any fur. Instead they are covered with a soft fuzz that you can't really see but you can feel. They don't even have whiskers!

Q. What do you call a cat that has eaten a whole duck?

A. A duck-filled fatty puss!

Unique Breeds

Munchkin

The munchkin is a medium-sized cat with very short legs. It is sometimes called the dachshund of cats.

Manx cats can be born with no tail (called "rumpy"), a small lump instead of a tail (called "stumpy") or a regular tail (called "longy").

Manx

Ears

Cats have excellent hearing. They can hear high-pitched sounds even better than a dog can. They are not as good with low-pitched sounds.

Eyes

Cats have 3 eyelids. The one closest to the eye is called the "haw." It acts much like a windshield wiper, sweeping dirt off the eyeball.

Q. Why did the cat sit on the computer?

A. To keep an eye on the mouse.

Because cats are most active at night, their eyes work best in dim light. Cats have much better night vision than humans do but can't see as well as we can in bright light.

Cats also have a special layer in their eye, called the tapetum. This layer helps reflect light back into the eye, so the cat can see in the dark. When you see light shining off a cat's eyes in the dark, it is because of the tapetum.

Nose

Cats have a great sense of smell. When they are born, it is their strongest sense. Newborn kittens are blind and deaf. They must use their sense of smell to find their mom so they can eat.

Q. What happened when the cat ate a clown fish?

A. It felt funny!

A cat's nose print is unique, just like our fingerprints.

The skin on a cat's nose is called nose leather.

Whiskers

A cat's whiskers help her feel her way around. They can pick up even the tiniest change in air movement, so the cat knows if something is in her way, even in the dark.

Cats don't just have whiskers on their snouts; they also have them above their eyes, on their chins and on the backs of their front legs.

A cat's tongue is rough. It is covered with tiny spines that are made of keratin, the same thing your fingernails are made from. These spines help the cat pull meat off bones. They also help the cat clean its fur and break up any mats in its coat.

Kittens have 26 baby teeth. They lose these teeth when they are about 4 months old. Adult cats have 30 teeth.

Cats don't chew their food. They use their sharp molars to bite off chunks and swallow them whole.

Q. What is a cat's favourite dessert?

A. Mag-pie!

Paws

Cats can pull their claws back into their feet when they aren't using them. This helps keep the claws nice and sharp and lets the cat walk quietly.

Q. What game did the cat want to play with the mouse?

A. Catch.

Most cats have 5 toes on each front paw and 4 toes on each back paw. Some cats are born with extra toes. Cats with extra toes are called polydactyl cats.

Tail

A cat uses its tail to help it balance, especially when walking on a narrow surface like a fence.

Q. Where did the cat go when it lost its tail?

A. To the re-tail store!

Cats also use their tails to "speak" to each other. When a cat is happy, its tail points straight up. If the cat is mad, its tail swishes back and forth.

A male cat's tail is usually a bit longer than a female's.

Behaviour

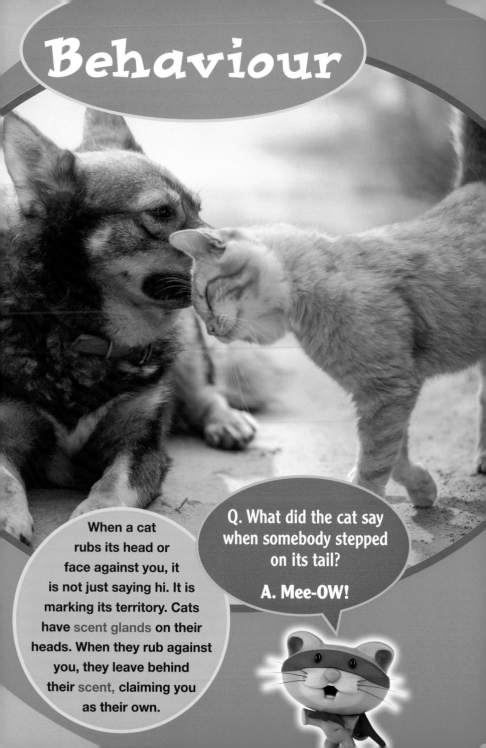

When a cat rubs its head or face against you, it is not just saying hi. It is marking its territory. Cats have scent glands on their heads. When they rub against you, they leave behind their scent, claiming you as their own.

Q. What did the cat say when somebody stepped on its tail?

A. Mee-OW!

Cats love to scratch. It is a natural behaviour for both wild and domestic cats. Scratching helps keep your kitty's claws clean and razor sharp.

Cats also scratch to mark their territory. Cats also have scent glands in their paws. As they scratch, they leave their scent on whatever they are scratching.

You can tell a lot about your cat's mood just by looking at her.

An angry cat's ears lay flat against its head.

Moods

If a cat is purring, it's happy, right? Not necessarily.

Cats purr when they are scared or in pain, too. It may be a way for them to comfort themselves.

Scientists believe that the rumbling noise of a cat's purr can help its cuts and broken bones heal faster.

A cat purrs while breathing in and out. The other noises it makes, like meowing or hissing, only happen when the cat breathes out.

Kittens

Q. What do baby cats wear?

A. Dia-purrs!

When a kitten is born, it is helpless. It can't move, see or hear. Its eyes are closed, and its ears are folded down against its head.

A kitten's eyes open when it is about 2 weeks old. It can't see properly, until it is about 10 weeks old.

All kittens are born with blue eyes. The eyes change to their adult colour when the kittens are 12 weeks old.

By the time the kitten is 3 weeks old, its ears can stand straight up and it can hear.

Once their eyes are open, kittens are curious to explore the world around them. But they cannot walk yet. They can only crawl on their bellies.

Newborn kittens spend most of their time curled up together to stay warm. If they get too cold, they can get sick.

On the Move

Grooming

Q. What did the cobbler say to the cat?

A. Shoe (shoo)!

Cats do a good job of keeping their bodies clean, but they need a little help.

A cat uses its rough tongue to pull free any loose fur. It swallows the fur and then throws up the hairball.

Brushing your cat about once a week, to help her swallow less fur and get fewer hairballs.

Most cats don't like and don't need baths, but there are some exceptions. Many of the hairless breeds need baths, and some old or sick kitties might need them, too.

Teeth and Claws

An important part of caring for your cat is keeping his claws trimmed.

When claws get too long, they can get caught on things and split. This really hurts your cat. They can also curve back and hurt the cat's paw pads.

Litter Box Care

Cats are clean creatures. When they go to the bathroom, it is natural for them to bury it in sand. That is why it is easy to train a cat to use a litter box. But there are rules you should follow to keep your kitty happy.

Cats do not like a dirty litter pan. Make sure you scoop it as least once per day and change the litter once a week.

If you have more than one cat, each cat needs its own pan.

Make sure the litter pan is not close to your cat's food or its bed.

If keeping the litter pan clean seems like too much work, you could train your cat to use the toilet. Kitty won't flush when he's done, though.

Q. What do cats like on their fish sticks?

A. Catsup.

Onion and garlic are toxic to cats. Even a little can damage a cat's blood. Watch out for prepared foods that might have onion or garlic in them, like pasta sauces, sausage and deli meats.

Nuts and other foods that are high in fat (like fat trimmed off a pork chop or steak) can give your cat a disease called pancreatitis, which can be fatal.

Unsafe Treats

Q. What is a kitty's favourite chocolate bar?

A. Kit Kat!

As they grow up, cats lose their ability to digest milk. A little bit of cheese now and then may be okay, but do not give your kitty milk to drink. She could get a stomach ache and diarrhea.

Caffeine is also bad for cats. If your kitty takes a few laps of coffee, tea, hot chocolate, pop or an energy drink, she will probably be okay, just a little hyper. But too much caffeine kill a cat.

Safe Treats

Q. What is a cat's favourite vegetable?

A. As-purr-agus!

Cats are obligate carnivores. This means that they need only meat to stay healthy. The best foods to give your kitty as a treat are cooked meat and eggs. But don't use salt, pepper or other seasonings on them.

Cats can't taste sweet flavours, so they are not interested in fruit. You could try carrots, asparagus, broccoli or green beans, but chances are your kitty won't eat them.

Cooked whole grains, like brown rice, are another safe choice. Cats don't need grains in their diet to be healthy, but small amounts won't make them sick.

Poisonous Plants

Although they eat meat, some cats like to chew on grasses and plants. Because they can't digest plants, they throw them up. This helps clean out your kitty's stomach.

Some plants, are poisonous for cats. Make sure all the plants in your house are safe. If your cat goes outside, make sure there are no toxic plants in your yard or garden.

Watch out for flowers or plants that are brought in for special occasions. Spring tulips, Easter lilies and poinsettias at Christmas are toxic to cats.

Cat grass is a safe choice. You can buy it pet stores.

Cats are not easy to train, like dogs are. You will never see a police cat chasing a criminal or a search and rescue cat looking through rubble. But that doesn't mean cats can't have jobs.

Many farmers keep barn cats to catch mice and other creatures that can damage their crops.

Working Cats

Cat Myths

Cats are loners

People often think that cats would rather be alone, but it's not true. Cats like company from their owners and can make friends with other cats or even other animals. They do like to hunt alone, though.

Q. What do you get when you cross a cat with a lemon.

A. A sour puss!

Cats can't get stuck in trees

If it can climb up, it can climb down, right? Wrong.

Cats claws point backwards, so they can climb up trees but not down. If they tried to climb down headfirst, the claws would slip out of the wood, and they would fall.

Cats have to climb down backwards, but many cats are too afraid because it is not natural for them.

The Publisher: iThink Books

Library and Archives Canada Cataloguing in Publication

Pirk, Wendy, 1973–, author
    Laugh out loud: cats / Wendy Pirk.

ISBN 978-1-897206-17-1 (softcover), 978-1-897206-18-6 (epub)

    1. Cats—Juvenile humor. 2. Cats—Miscellanea—Juvenile literature. 3. Canadian wit and humor (English)—Juvenile literature. 4. Wit and humor, Juvenile. I. Title. II. Title: Cats

PN6231.C23P57 2017   jC818'.602   C2017-906356-1

Front cover credits: s_derevianko/Thinkstock.

Back cover credits: krblokhin/Thinkstock; Photodisc/Thinkstock; kozorog/Thinkstock.

Photo credits: Every effort has been made to accurately credit the sources of photographs and illustrations. Any errors or omissions should be reported directly to the publisher for correction in future editions. *From Thinkstock:* adamdowdee282, 53; AdrianDavies, 55; akinshin, 21; Aksenovko, 59; AlbinaTiplyashina, 52; Aletakae, 22b; AllaSaa, 58; AlonsoAguilar, 44; arosoft, 25b; Astrid860, 41a; BendeBruyn, 39a; callofthewild, 7a; Chalabala, 55b; CoreyFord, 3; cynoclub, 15, 51; darkbird77, 26; Darya_Mamulchenko, 29; derevianko, 12a; Donald34, 24; Ed-Ni-Photo, 35; fermate, 41b; fotoedu, 50; fotokate, 63a; GlobalP, 5, 20; gutaper, 13b; iculizard, 8; igaguri_1, 11; Ingram publishing, 30; InvisibleNature, 27; janekub, 23a; Jevtic, 43; jph9362, 36; Jupiterimages, 16; kicia_papuga, 57; koldunova, 40; kozorog, 25a; krblokhin, 14; LindaJohnsonbaugh, 19; MarieHolding, 6; martYmage, 7b; MontyPeter, 47; MW47, 46; okeanas, 62; ollegN, 49b; Page Light Studios, 13a; PatrikSlezak, 45; PeteGallop, 9a; PhotoAllel, 23b; Photodisc, 28; RobFranklin, 9b; Roolvan, 54; rukawajung, 10, 31; Rulles, 2; S_Kazeo, 49a; Seregraff, 18, 22a, 32; Shirinov, 56; sjallenphotography, 37; socreative_media, 12b; Suemack, 61; TheKoRp, 34; totophotos, 4; virgonira, 63b; vladans, 42; vvvita, 38, 39b; wildcat78, 17; y-studio, 48; Zasili, 60.

Animal Illustrations: julos/Thinkstock.

We acknowledge the financial support of the Government of Canada.
Nous reconnaissons l'appui financier du gouvernement du Canada.

Alberta ∎
Government

Funded by the Government of Canada | Canada
Financé par le gouvernement du Canada

Produced with the assistance of the Government of Alberta, Alberta Media Fund.

PC: 38